A Quick Guide to Machine Gun Maintenance

Glenn Fleming M.O.D.

ISBN: 978-1-7330053-2-6

Dedication

The author (me) wishes to thank all the people that have helped write this book. Without them, and there are many, I wouldn't have been able to do it.

That having been said any shortcomings in it are mine, and mine alone.

I also want to thank all the customers I've had over the years. Thank you for entrusting me with your "babies".

The legal BS. The author takes no responsibility for any damage you may do to yourself, others, or property attempting to work on any gun using this as a guide. Basically, gunsmith at your own risk!

Lastly as I've always wanted to write a novel so let me start with,

Once Upon a Time in the Old West....

Introduction

I'm currently sitting here, at 32,000 feet in the air, flying across the Pacific on my way back home to the states from Thailand. The rest of the people in the aircraft have no idea I'm about to 'pen' a book on how to service machine guns and I'm sure if they knew half of them would be terrified and the other half would think I'm insane. I'm willing to bet all of them would secretly want to shoot the things I'm going to be talking about!

A few days ago, I was reading a small paperback book on gunsmithing the single action revolver. My wife noticed and said I should write a book on machine guns and other NFA weapon gunsmithing. To be sure there aren't any books of the type out there, and I routinely get emails or calls asking if I take in apprentices. Adding to it, there are no places-save the military-where one can learn to gun-smith on fully automatic weapons. And even then, smithing will still be limited to current generation weapons. After all, there aren't too many militaries using Maxims or MG34s!

This book won't be all inclusive; there are a couple as-sumptions that need to be made. First, knowledge of safe handling of weapons is a must! Second, a good knowledge of the mechanics of weapons. Third, that the smith is not an idiot. These things are assumed both for liability reasons and so writing out a book equivalent to war and peace can be avoided. After all my typing sucks and I want to finish this before I die! Finally, this book is envisioned as the start of a series on machine guns. Think of it as a general guide.

So, let's get to it shall we! I, your friendly Merchant of Death, will guide you through the wonderful world of machine guns and give you the keys to true happiness!

Glenn Fleming M.O.D.

04-20-19

1 CONTENTS

The MP43/STG44

OK Damnit...... The 1919

The most beautiful gun in the world, the MG34

The 1918 BAR

Test fire

Dealing with the unknown

CHAPTER 1

THE MECHANICS OF OPERATION

If you are reading this, it will be taken for granted that you have at least a passible interest in weaponry. Things like Blow Back, and Gas Operation should be familiar. There are, of course others but there aren't too many bolt action and single action machine guns (I'm working on the latter as we speak). The latter currently being developed by yours truly.

But do you know of delayed roller blowback? How about the various locking systems bolts employ? That's where the machine gunsmith, for lack of a better term, differs from the gunsmith working on a bolt action or single action. There are literally a ton of different actions and lock ups even in the same type of mechanic operation.

Take for example the STG44. The gun uses a gas operation system as does the AK74. Most folks not "in the know" would think that because of outward appearances they would operate the same. In fact, save for the gas operation portion that would not be the case. The STG uses a drop down lock up system and the AK uses a rotating bolt lock up system. In addition, the fire control groups (FCG) are completely different.

On the LH side we see the AK bolt, on the RH side the STG 44 bolt. They are in fact completely different!

Blow Back Operation

Starting with the easiest of the bunch, blowback. At its heart the blowback operated machine gun is nothing more than "every action has an equal and opposite reaction." The cartridge is pushed into the chamber, usually by spring pressure where a fixed firing pin hits the primer and fires the round. When the round goes off it imparts forces in both directions. One side firing the bullet out the barrel and the other making the bolt or slide travel to the rear. Usually there is a single sear surface in the FCG that reacts with a corresponding sear surface on the bolt. Easy enough right? And some are but most are not.

When working on these types of machine guns, the first thing that must be realized is that it has a greater than normal chance of an out of battery. The reason being is the fixed firing pin in most of them.

If the round is stripped from the mag and the cartridge does not get completely chambered the round may still go off, out of battery. Usually this happens with the smaller submachine guns and doesn't present to much of a problem EXCEPT for the potential for eye damage. Shall we look at a popular gun and break down a problem?

Blow Back Problems

The MP40 is a very popular blowback that is simplicity itself. There is a bolt with a sear surface and, a corresponding sear surface in the FCG, that's it. No disconnector, no semi auto, nothing. Let's say we are getting stove pipes, a problem I particularly hate as it could be one of a couple of things or a combination of things.

As you must pick a spot to start let's confirm that the action isn't dragging. Work the bolt by hand while engaging the trigger on an UNLOADED gun and see if you can detect any dragging or excessive movement of the bolt. Dragging, unless very slight, would be self-evident and excessive movement would equate side to side or up and down wiggling that makes the bolt slow down when chambering a round. Remember there is nothing more than spring pressure responsible for loading and firing the round so any drag will prevent the gun from firing.

Since we are talking stove piping, we will say all is cool with that check.

The next thing would be to check the ejector. Each ejector on a gun has a specific direction that it throws the cases. This is the angle that it's beveled at and if it's off, which can happen from wear, can throw the cases out in a weird angle or even back into the gun. An easy way to check this is with dummy rounds. Load a couple up and cycle by hand to see the ejection angle. You, of course, also want to check for any damage to the part as well.

Pictured above the MP40 Ejector (the part hanging over the mag-well). Notice it is nice and flat on its face

We will say that looks ok too. Did I mention that I hate stove piping?

Next, we can check the extractor. If this is not working, it may not have enough tension to hold the round on its way to the ejector OR have too much play thus affecting the angle that the round hits the ejector. And easy way to check is to break out our dummy rounds and with the bolt out of the gun, pop a dummy in the face of the bolt and check the hold. You can also push up on the extractor to check tension but that's kind of an arbitrary thing unless it's very loose. Check for any additional damage.

We checked that and that looks fine as well; just fuck.

Since we have checked all the parts of the gun for damage and found none. We need to check the operation of key components and determine if they are good. We need to be a little more investigative and turn our sights to the chamber

Damage or imperfections in the chamber are two big reasons for stove piping. What happens is the chamber gets fouled with something or physically scratched and when the case expands in the chamber upon firing it tends to grab onto the imperfection slowing everything down. So, we have our little flashlight and behold a burr in the chamber! Obviously placed there by an angry god. We break out the chamber hone; give it a quick who's your daddy and presto the thing works again.

Now admittedly this is a simple gun to work on, but the most important thing we did here was take things one step at a time. You will need to do this with every problem that comes to you. I find if I try to shotgun blast a problem and tackle too many things at once; the small stuff which caused the problem in the first place tends to get over looked.

Well that was fun! Now should we complicate things.

The Sten gun is probably one of, if not, the ugliest guns around. Made from a muffler pipe, bed spring, a couple pieces of metal and a bolt, it's a miracle the damn thing works at all. But work it does and usually quite well. A big part of where it differs from the MP40, other than its uglier, is that it has a provision for semi-automatic fire. This can be done by pushing the button on the side of the gun. When semi-automatic fire is selected a small finger of flat metal (disconnector) is pushed upwards and when hit by the correct spot on the bolt during recoil it forces the sear to engage the sear on the bolt and hold it back for the follow up shot when the trigger is pulled.

A runaway gun is a gun that continues to fire after the trigger has been let go or, when set in semi-automatic mode fires full auto.

For our purposes we will address this malfunction when the gun is in the semi-automatic mode. (Though you can have a runaway in full auto as well I would like to involve as many factors as possible in the malfunction.)

Much to our surprise the gun continues to fire in fully automatic mode and to make matters worse it does it with the trigger not depressed at all! Deciding that the smart idea would be to "put it to bed" we return to the shop to see what is wrong with our beloved ugly stick.

As with the MP40 example our first course of action is to see if the gun operates correctly when hand cycling. One of the ways it could be doing this is if the gun is short stroking, meaning the bolt does not return far enough to engage the sear. It turns out that it functions fine though in as much as the bolt slides smoothly back and forth in the receiver. The trouble is its still in semi and it shouldn't be sliding back and forth like a proper machine gun.

Our hopes for an easy fix are dashed.

Pressing on we then disassemble the weapon down to its major components including taking off the cover on the FCG.

Initial inspection shows that the bolt is good to go as well as the receiver tube. The recoil spring is of the correct length and "stoutness" showing it not to be broken or mangled. We then look to the FCG. Turning it over we can see a loose spring that should be attached to something. We also find another larger diameter spring that is somewhat loose in its area of operation. Upon closer inspection we notice that the long smaller diameter spring has broken in half and one-half lays on the trigger and one-half lies on the larger diameter spring. We immediately call a parts supplier and order a new spring and in 7-10 days make the repair!

Here you can see the long spring attached to the trigger

Now admittedly this was quite a simple fix. With the smaller spring taking tension off the disconnector hold down spring, there was no positive action by the disconnector. The main thing I wanted to get across here is the runaway issue. Here I treat the runaway as no big deal but that's not the case at all. If you aren't prepared for a runaway, especially with a larger caliber violent gun like an HK51 the outcome could, for lack of a better word, suck, a lot! Something else to think about. If you happen to work at a range that does machinegun rentals the person shooting may have zero full auto time and a runaway even on something as small an MP5 may ruin everyone's day.

Speaking of MP5s shall we talk a little about the roller lock guns?

CHAPTER 2

THE ROLLER LOCK MECHANISM

The MP5 and its delayed roller cousins the HK33, G3 and even the STG57 operate on a system that incorporates flutes cut into the chamber to help with extraction. Basically, when the bolt travels forward the rollers go out and lock the bolt head into position into the trunnion. This is accomplished when the bolt body, under spring pressure, rams the locking shoulder between the rollers. When the round is fired, these do not have a fixed firing pin by the way, unlocking does not immediately take place. Instead unlocking is delayed until gas pressure has dropped to a safe level in the barrel. This is accomplished by the locked bolt head staying in place until recoil energy hits the carrier with enough force to drive it rearward thus moving the locking shoulder back and unlocking the rollers. Also, a small amount of gas enters the flutes in the chamber and aids extraction. This has the advantage of firing from a closed bolt regarding accuracy. It does make for a dirtier weapon overall especially when running suppressed. That having been said this is a time tested and proved weapon. There are a couple things to watch out for on these guns though. The first thing is that when the flutes become full of crud it can make the weapon not fire correctly. Problems ranging from non-extraction to failure to feed can result.

They do make chamber flute brushes and if you intend to work on these type guns, I recommend you buy some.

Another thing is headspace is not obtained in the traditional sense. Instead the measurement of bolt gap comes into play. I do recommend getting the manuals for any weapon system you intend to work on but as an example the bolt gap on an MP5 reads between .010 and .020 with optimum being .018. This measurement is taken between the bolt head and bolt carrier in the firing position with the hammer down.

The bolt and carrier for the MP5. Bolt gap is checked in the gap between the head and carrier body. Of course, it needs to be in the gun!

Also, the FCG on an MP5 is vastly different from the FCG on an open bolt submachine gun. Instead these mechanisms will have a set of components that will essentially time the hammer to only drop when the bolt is in the fully locked position. If the timing is off on this what usually happens is the hammer "follows" the carrier and bolt into the battery position and you get light primer strikes.

That covers the main types of blow back weapons systems you will probably see in submachineguns. There are others such as the MG34 and MG42 but those are a gas assisted type and will be addressed later. Now we turn our attention to a more complex type operation. The Gas Operated machine gun.

CHAPTER 3

GAS OPERATED MACHINE GUNS

The gas operated machine gun does nothing more than harness the gasses from firing the round to cycle the weapon. This is accomplished mostly by drilling a port in the barrel of the weapon to tap the gasses. Notable gas operated systems would be the AK47 or M4.

All gas operated weapons (that I know of anyway) have some form of locking bolt. This is done by a twisting bolt head (M4), a tilting bolt (STG44), flaps that expand outward (RPD), or some other type of locking system. The reason to lock the bolt is twofold. First it provides a small margin of safety. As these shoot bigger rounds than the submachineguns it's important to let some of the recoil energy dissipate down the barrel. Second, and perhaps more importantly with the bolt locked more gas pressure can be used to cycle the system of the gun.

The tapped gasses hit a gas piston of some type that works the carrier in a rearward movement. This in turn unlocks the bolt and recoil begins.

Top; M4 bolt showing its locking lugs. Bottom: The shoulder on the AK bolt locks the bolt against the corresponding area in the front trunnion.

SAMPLE GAS OPERATED GUN PROBLEMS

Let's look at a simple problem with a gas operated M240

When firing an M240 there is a sudden stoppage. The bolt is closed (this is an open bolt weapon but still locks via a drop down bolt) and there upon pulling the bolt back you see it is hard to pull the charging handle to the rear and the round in the chamber was fired.

Off to the shop we go.

After inspecting the fired case you note there are not indications of a fouled chamber scratches, gouges, dents, etc.

The bolt when allowed to cycle forward is still hard to charge to the rear. However, the FCG mechanism seems to operate as it is supposed to. A closer barrel inspection notes that the chamber is indeed just fine. After looking at the gas lug on the barrel you note there is carbon fouling and it is set to max.

We can see the gas setting set to "2" which is the middle setting

After removing the buttstock, recoil assembly, and bolt/carrier you note there is significant carbon fouling on the forward section of the gas piston. A closer inspection of the gas tube indicates the same with a lot of carbon on the inside of the gas tube walls.

Basically, the weapon had at some point demonstrated carbon fouling and instead of being cleaned the gas system was turned up until it could no longer be turned up and overcome the fouling. This essentially "stuck" the gas piston. There may have been some initial movement but not enough to cycle the weapon.

This happens more often than you would think, and I've seen a ton of this type of failure come in. It's not hard to fix but is time consuming. For the most part a dunk in Butches Bore Shine for a few hours loosens the carbon then a little elbow grease and you are good to go. Occasionally you will get a gun that has this problem but has been firing corrosive ammo. This will make you curse your choice of profession and just in general hate life.

Let's look at another gas operated weapon system issue that will rear its ugly head from time to time.

Each gun has its own amount of gas that it requires to operate it. Sometimes that though, there are problems with the amount of gas going into the gun to work the action. This is known as either under or over gassing. Under gassing will basically give you a bolt action and over gassing can beat the gun to death. Not really what you want in your $25,000 M16!

Under gassing repair is generally easier to deal with. After all its much easier to drill a hole than replace a barrel.

If your gun is over gassed you could weld and redrill a gas port on a gun that has an oversize port but given the choice, it's better to go with a barrel change.

First under gassing:

Tapped gas pressure needs to be enough to overcome spring pressure and parts friction to cycle the weapon. Sometimes the factory hole in the barrel is undersized, may have some trash in it, or it's not even drilled all the way through.

Indicators of this problem are basically "my gun no workie".

It can be anything from slow rate of fire, short stroking, to being basically a bolt action. This can be incredibly frustrating. Most folks always assume the factory barrel/gas block to be good and will look at damn near everything else first.

The true hell is that you have wasted a ton of time on other stuff when all you had to do was drill a small hole!

Now let's tackle Over Gassing

This one is kind of sneaky because usually the gun is working. Trouble is its working to good. Really the only symptom you may get of this is an extremely high rate of fire. Like when your sweet little PKM is firing at MG42 speed that's over gassing and in the case of the PKM, and others, it will tear your gun up.

Let's use the People Killing Machine as an example. This is probably the finest General-Purpose Machine Gun (GPMG) ever made. They run and run and run. The issue is the type of metal in the receivers, especially the receivers made in the states. They work well to be sure, but they are a bit brittle, so you can expect cracks to appear in them. The fix for this is a very involved process that I may address in another book.

Anyway, you are shooting your PKM and notice its fast ROF after that last barrel change everyone digs it and it does sound cool, so you continue firing.

Bear in mind the PKM doesn't have a buffer to speak of other than a small solid puck, so all that recoil energy is basically being downloaded right into your rear trunnion. In other words, it's taking a beating. There is an important part to remember when servicing older machine guns or parts kits-built guns.

The springs you are using in them are SURPLUS parts i.e. they have had the dogshit shot out of them!

That means it takes less recoil/gas force to get a complete cycle. This also means it's not as good at buffering the blow to the gun.

So, with all that in mind guess what happens in short order? Yep cracks, most often in the rear trunnion and the area over the ejection door.

These are fixable but are an absolute pain in the ass.

Having said all that, the fix for the PKM is usually to just adjust the gas setting at the gas port. Other guns like the M4 may need a new barrel or an adjustable gas block, if available. Still others like the SCAR series will use a small gas jet that can be removed and replaced with jets of different size to adjust gas.

Summary

We have covered the two main mechanisms you are likely to meet, blow back and gas operation. Now let's cover something that incorporates a bit of both. I don't really know if there is an official name for it, but I'll call it Gas Assisted Delayed Blow back. These would be your

MG42, MG34 (my favorite), and MG15 type weapons. I'll discuss the 42 and the 34 here without getting into the operation of every component. We will cover that in more detail later.

CHAPTER 4

MG42 FUNCTION

The Mg42 uses a booster/nozzle set up that traps the gas expelled by the fired round between the booster and face of the nozzle. Using that gas, it pushes the barrel, and locked bolt rearwards to unlock the bolt and initial recoil (bolt movement to the rear). This is a cool little setup and as you can tell works quite well.

Here we see the barrel, nozzle, booster, and flash hider lay out in as they are in the gun

Now there are more parts to this type of mechanism to return the barrel to battery, but that just gives us more stuff to fix when it breaks right!

Time for an MG42 malfunction!

You take your 42 out to the range dressed to impress! You have a ton of rounds and you are going to rock it. You set up pull the trigger and it runs like hell. Belt after belt you tinker with it but just can't figure out what's wrong. You take it home to fight with it on the bench.

Now here is where I'm going to shamelessly plug a friend of mine AND save you a ton of time. If you find yourself working on German WWII guns you NEED to buy the German manuals that are translated by one John Baum. He has a ton of them ranging all the way up to, I shit you not, the 8.8 Flak! These manuals cover all aspects of the gun and will save you time. And time is money.

So, having referenced Johns' books we can see one test we can try is the "pogo" test. You take off the flash hider and booster, turn the gun upside down and push down on it. It should sit on the face of the nozzle with no drop and bounce back up from the recuperator spring pressure when pushed down. If it does not you have found the issue and by God, you are just going to have the best time!

The Mg42 recuperator is a small stamped metal tube with flats on it. It is installed under the rail on the LH side of the gun. Its sole function is to return the barrel to battery. You will need to remove it and check/change springs.

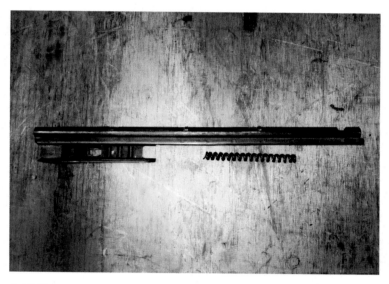

MG42 recuperator and a spring. Note, there are 4 springs in the recuperator

WARNING: This not an easy thing to do and the springs in it are under a lot of pressure so be careful.

When rebuilding a recuperator you will need good springs. I bought a couple recuperators and took them apart to harvest the springs. Basically, I just use the longest ones.

The springs in the recuperator have a rod with a flat head, kind of like a nail with no point that top them off. Above that, in the little square opening, is a small piece of flat metal with a hole in it. You need to press down on the "nail" and spring and turn the small flat to remove it from the hole.

My method is to take an AK cleaning rod and push down through the hole in the flat onto the "nail" head. Once that's done insert a small flathead screwdriver between the flat and the nail head. Then pull back on the screwdriver and remove the cleaning rod. While holding the screwdriver back, take needle nose pliers and turn the flat until it can be removed. Trust me it's a pain in the ass.

There are a few other types of machine gun mechanisms out there, take the mini gun for instance, but they aren't as prevalent as the ones we have discussed. Also, it should be noted that other guns use these actions. The 1919 uses a gas assisted blow back and the M2 is basically a closed bolt blow back where the bolt locks via a bolt locking bar that raises from the bottom.

The point being there are many different actions out there with different lock ups. I'm not going to go into each of them as I'm not writing War and Peace, but Johns manuals should give you a good starting point.

CHAPTER 5

BUILDING A MACHINE GUN FROM A PARTS KIT

Not everyone can afford a transferable machinegun. Hell, I know I can't, so a handy alternative, provided you have the correct licensing, is to build a gun from a parts kit.

My aim is to guide you in how to figure things out. Not as much as an "insert tab A into slot B" if you catch my meaning.

First and foremost, if you can find a saw cut kit buy it. They are becoming more of a rarity.

Most parts kits however are of the torch cut variety. Meaning some big old mean man somewhere took a cutting torch to a perfectly good machine gun and chopped it all up. It sucks but usually isn't as bad as it seems. Now days they cut the barrel too diabolical bastards!!

Say we have a PPs43 that needs to be functional again. In this instance you can figure that you will need donor receiver metal, a barrel, trunnion with plate and rivets, a homemade jig to keep the barrel straight and of course a kit.

Typical PPs43 Parts kit layout

The way most PPs43 kits came in is with the receiver torch cut towards the rear, middle, and shroud section with the middle section being thrown away. Therefore, you will need the donor section of the receiver.

Luckily all the parts you will need are readily available, except for an alignment jig (hence the" home made" part).

The first thing you will want to do is lay everything out to make sure it's all there. Bolt, recoil rod assembly, receiver sections, lower receiver, pin that hold in the barrel and the pin that holds the lower and upper, rear sight, and a mag if your kit includes one.

33

Once you're satisfied you have everything you will want to order the parts you will need. As I've said they are

1. Barrel
2. Receiver part(s)
3. Trunnion with plate and rivets
4. Ammo (you will want that later!!)

You can get all this stuff from various sources. The sources change but aren't too hard to find online.

The next thing to do is to get your receiver parts and clean them up. They often have Cosmoline on them so clean that off with diesel or break cleaner. I usually try to get off the slag from the torch cut with a little help from a Dremel and a chisel. You will want good clean metal and no slag when you weld it up. If you do attempt to weld with "dirty" metal, you will run into porosity. Meaning there are voids in the weld. The only corrective action for this is to grind out the weld and start over.

After all the slag is gone blast all the parts. You can use beads or aluminum oxide it just depends on the final finish. I tend to Duracoat all mine, so I use the AO for a more "grippy" finish.

Once you are satisfied all the parts are cleaned up, and your barrel is in, you can lay everything out and start to see the relation of all the parts. More often than not you won't find any kind of measurement data online, so you must make it up as it goes. Basically, you use the existing good parts to set your distances.

For example, taking the lower receiver we can discover our distances needed. We know the front hole on the lower receiver is the attachment point for the rear hole on the trunnion area of the upper. So, we can put that in that area. The barrel will set your distance for the front shroud and the rear of the lower will set the distance for the rear of the upper receiver. This means all you must do is "fill in the blanks". It sounds easy, and it is, but it does involve math.

Each kit is a little different so there is no way I can give you numbers, but you should be able to figure it out from the example above.

Using our donor receiver, we just weld in the sections missing. The receiver body is easy you can make a short rod section of aluminum to use as a backer for the weld and to keep the parts in line. You can use the bolt to keep it in-line, but I don't recommend it. Make the rod the EXACT size as the inside of the receiver tube and clamp two sections together. Tack it together and let it cool. Check the alignment and weld up using copper backers on the welded sections. I weld a section and let it cool before welding another. That way if there is a slight twist due to cooling, I can weld the opposite area to try to bring it back in. Once you are satisfied with the results move on to the next section and finish out the rear of the receiver. Moving on to the forward section we can use the trunnion plate to set out distance there and for the rivets. Weld the plate to the receiver using spot welds. Once your trunnion is in move to the shroud section.

Here I build a jig about 4-5" long that has steps in it. One step is the size of the ID of the barrel. The next is the size of the ID of the end of the shroud with a flat that presses against the shroud. The distance between the flat on the front of the shroud and the flat on the front of the barrel sets my shroud distance. I use small pieces of copper flat inside the shroud as backers then tack just like before. Once everything is tacked and looks good, I weld it up.

Once all the welds are cleaned up, reinstall the barrel this time with the holding pin. Assemble the upper to lower, again with the pin and test function WITHOUT any ammo.

Once everything works well, test fire to see how it functions. If you have some rubbing issues, and you probably will, use blue lay out to see where the rubbing is and remove/add metal where needed being careful to not remove too much

Once everything is good to go 'in the white" so to speak, coat and have fun!

You can use this same kind of technique with any kit, utilizing the existing parts to set your spacing.

For the guns that require a set headspace you will need to get some headspace gages and use those when setting the area for headspace.

For example, the RPD has flaps that lock into the sides of the receiver.

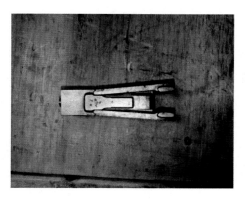

Bottom view of an RPD bolt the "flaps" are what locks the bolt in position.

Usually you will need to weld the area between the barrel mounting area and the flap lock. Assemble the sections, with the bolt installed, flaps engaged in the corresponding area of the receiver with a go headspace gage installed.

This will set your headspace. Bear in mind there will be shrinkage when you weld up the parts, so you may have to adjust your headspace by inserting a piece of tape between the back of the headspace gage and the front of the bolt face. It will all depend on how much heat and weld it takes to get your parts together.

Now here is my disclaimer on all this:

Building up a kit into a machine gun can be dangerous as hell. If you don't know what you are doing don't do it. This guide is a reference on techniques that have worked for me, but it certainly has been trial and error. Have I screwed up? You bet. Everything I make or work on gets test fired by me. If there is anyone going to get hurt, I much prefer it to be me. Remember these things aren't toys and they need to be treated like they aren't as well!

CHAPTER 6

THE THINGS YOU WILL WORK ON

In this area we are going over the stuff that you WILL see as a "machinegun smith". These are the guns that everyone has and often break due to the fact they are run hard. They are good guns, which is why everyone owns them, but due to the shear amount of them out there you will see them. Guns like the MP5, MG42, AK47, M4, 1919, M2 50 Cal, Thompson (1928 model), 1918 BAR and PPSH41 to name a few.

There are, like I said, a ton of these guys out there and they are great weapons, but they will break, and you will see them so if you are serious about working on MG's you need to know them. I'm not going to go over everything that can go wrong with them since I'm tired of typing and it's time for a drink. I will go over some of the more common things I've seen to hopefully help you out along the way.

Always remember though, don't be afraid to use your hammer!

THE MP5

We discussed in a previous chapter the roller locking mechanism of the MP5 and its siblings, so I won't rehash that here, but I will say this is by far one of the most sought after, popular transferable or post sample guns out there. If you do this for ANY length of time you will work on them. That having been said let's get the ball rolling.

Barrel change on an MP5

This is easy and hard all at the same time. In addition to the new barrel go ahead and buy a new barrel pin as well. I usually keep a couple pins, regular and oversize, always. When you remove them, they will break also your regular size pin may just fall through the hole it's supposed to fit tightly into so it's good to be prepared.

The first thing you will do is take the gun apart as far as possible. Once done its time to remove the pin. There are a couple ways to do this There are fancy pin drivers you use on a press (the best way) or you can just wail on it with a hammer (the cheap way). Either way the pin is probably going to break. So, depending on what you are more comfortable with and what equipment you have on hand will determine the method of pin removal.

Ill cover the hammer method as there are several differ-ent types of press but one basic type way to work a ham-mer.

You will want a starter punch (a broken punch with a short shaft that has been ground flat works great), a BFH (big fucking hammer), and something to secure the re-ceiver. That something to secure the receiver must be hard but soft enough that it doesn't screw your receiver up-wood or plastic blocks work great.

Lay your receiver, with the pin facing up, on your blocks. Make sure the receiver is level, supporting the rear of it as well. Take you BFH and your flat starter punch and take out some frustrations. You may get it to move first swing, but it will probably take a couple. Once it moves a bit, say 1/8" or so take a standard punch of the right size and continue wailing. Remember two things: keep your punch straight and have enough space below the receiver so the pin will come out!

Next remove the barrel. You will need to build a barrel press jig for this. I use an aluminum rod that has been turned down to the size of the ID of the chamber on one end for about ¾" and the rest is about 1/8" shy of the ID of the receiver. It, of course, needs to be long enough to press the barrel out of the receiver.

41

For this you will need a press. Although you can use a hammer there is a decent chance of really screwing up the receiver. Also, you bought one why not use it!

Put your receiver, barrel down, on the press plates. Insert your jig in the chamber and start pressing. It will probably make a loud "pop" sound when it starts moving. Trust me you will know when that is.

Grab the barrel as it comes out, more to save your press bar than the old barrel and remove.

Installing is a bit trickier. I put the barrels in the freezer overnight to shrink a bit. The next day Ill remove it and grease the trunnion and trunnion area of the barrel. Install it from the rear of the gun and start pressing it in. If you are lucky it will be smooth when it goes in. So far, I've never been lucky. Usually what I see is that it goes in jerky and makes bolt gapping a pain.

For bolt gap you are going to shoot for between .010" and .020" with .018" being best. Not a ton of room for screwing up.

You will basically have to press the barrel in, put the bolt in and check gap between the end of the bolt head and front of carrier as viewed from the bottom of the gun. HK makes a high-speed feeler just for this, but your basic feeler gage works great for this measurement.

Checking bolt gap on the MP5. You can see the feeler gage inserted here

This can be tedious but MUST be done right if you want the gun to fire!

Once you are satisfied with the gap you've set try it again with the gun together to check everything. If it's still good let it sit for a bit for the cold barrel to warm and "set" in the trunnion.

After waiting for the barrel to warm up drill the barrel pin hole, being careful not to go too hard or too fast as that could move the barrel. Insert the pin and PRESS in. I say press because any side to side movement of the pin and it will snap in half causing much cursing.

ROLLER CHANGE

Let's say you just need to set the bolt gap but don't really want to change the barrel. That's pretty easy to do! Just order more rollers and install. Of course, there is more to it than that!

MP5 bolt head lay out with the rollers in the locked position.

Bolt rollers lock the bolt head to the trunnion when firing the weapon, so you need to right size to set your bolt gap correctly otherwise it's the worst parts of the bible. In a nut shell, larger roller will increase your bolt gap while smaller rollers will decrease it. Easy right! There are a ton of different rollers made from -8 to +10 each set being a .010 size different from the last.

They are easy to change. For starters take the bolt head off the carrier. Next drive the small pin in the middle of the top of the bolt head down into the bolt head. Push the rollers out one direction and poof done. Installation is the reverse.

Of note is to mind the small spring or clip that holds the rollers in. Often when you remove the rollers you will find that it is broken. It's no big deal just replace as necessary.

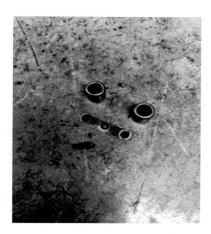

MP5 roller set up showing the rollers, clip that holds them in position and pin that holds the whole enchilada

Another critical feature of the roller locking HK series of guns is the locking shoulder. As I have previously mentioned, the locking shoulder actually "sets" the time that the bolt is locked to the trunnion. Normally, unless it's broken, you shouldn't have to change this. If you do have to change it, it's easy enough; I don't need to talk about it here. If you are wondering what locking piece to go with there are a ton of online references for your particular application. There will be some that aren't covered, such as the Scooby MP5/MP5k mix gun I made. On those you will have to pick a starting point and go from there. In the Scooby gun it was also necessary to adjust the length of the recoil spring and rod since it was made with parts from different guns. Long and short of that is sometimes you need to experiment to get things to work on custom weapons.

My daughters Scooby machine gun. The back half is MK5K the front half is MP5. When custom making weapons you sometimes need to custom make parts. In this case it was the recoil rod and spring. They are a custom length to fit and work in the gun.

CHAPTER 7

FURTHER MG42 PROBLEMS

There probably is no more iconic belt fed machine gun than the MG42. Its looks and definitely its sound are known to everyone. It's a gun that after you shoot for the first time there is a no doubt in your mind this is a weapon of war.

My particular gun has over 20k rounds though it and has only had a couple minor issues. Needless to say, I'm proud and happy about that.

Having said that, what are some of the issues you can expect to see on the MG42? I've already covered the recuperator so I'm not going to rehash that here. And parts breakage is simple to diagnose and fix so no need to cover that.

Other issues you are likely to see are a shortened recoil spring. The true length of the recoil spring is 16.9". A quick and dirty way to check the length of the spring is it should be the distance, with the rear sight extended down, from the end of the receiver to the end of the rear sight.

Another thing that will go bad over time is the hole in the booster or nozzle will get bigger through erosion. The booster hole size for an 8mm should be 11.5mm. You can

ID this by the gun running slowly. The reverse of this is the gun running WAY to fast. This I've seen from am MG3 nozzle in an 8mm gun. The difference is only .5mm but the speed that it goes is very impressive. Having said that it beats the gun to death so it's not good!

MG42 nozzle on top on MG3 nozzle below. Notice the ring around the MG3 nozzle

You may also find that one of the rails is messed up. Maybe a guide came loose or a dent or something. The rails are simple to install, l but you will need a backer tool. You can make or buy these by the way. Also, be aware the rails are not the same; they are either a left rail or a right rail. An easy way to tell is that the top will be slightly ground for the area of the feed tray.

You can see here the area that has been ground down for the feed tray area. This would be the LH rail.

Your camming piece (it's not a trunnion right John!) may go bad as well. Its again easy to replace but make sure both parts are MATCHING numbered. If not, nice paperweight.

Here we see an MG42 camming piece. Notice both parts are numbers matching

The gun is actually very easy to fix all the way around. Just pay attention to what it is telling you and go from there. If it's a slow rate of fire, chances are you have either a messed-up gas trap system or a burr somewhere. If something catastrophic happens say bolt roller breakage or sear breakage you will know as there won't be much firing after that happens!

It's not really a "fix" per say but I will address a jig I made to do rewelds. It's a simple channel of metal with holes drilled every inch so you can install long bolts. The bolts have a nut, large washer, another washer, and a wing nut. You arrange the receiver sections on the channel using the washers as holders (one top one bottom) till you get the desired spacing and height. Once this is done put copper backers into the sections, so you can weld. As for alignment side to side use a (long) straight edge or even some string to get things aligned. Tighten down the wingnuts, I mean really tighten down the wingnuts and build a machine gun.

A picture of the authors MG42 Jig. This is an early one that the bolts don't go all the way through. Note the rails are held in by small screws to align the rear receiver section

Incidentally if a client comes in with a partial reweld or a reweld that has never run right to fix I give you this advice. While it is cool to fix "the unfixable" there isn't really any money in it.

CHAPTER 8

THE AK47

Another stand out weapon that has withstood the test of time.

Hugo Schmeisser really knew what he was doing!!

I kid... Kinda.

To be honest one of the things you will see the most, fix wise, on these is that someone shot it with corrosive ammo and never cleaned it, yay.

If you are lucky someone will bring one in that they shot the hell out of doing mag dump after mag dump and melted the barrel. Yes, you can really do that!

The AK47 is a gas operated, rotating locking bolt, assault rifle. The "trip" to release the hammer, its hammer fired by the way, is on the inner RH side of the gun a bit behind the magwell.

Here the punch is pointing to the tip of the full auto trip

It is a simple arm that when acted upon by the tab on the carrier moves the trip out of the way allowing the hammer to fall and fire the round. This works the same way in semi or full auto. What sets the action of full or semi in the gun, after you have selected it is the safety lever acting upon the tabs on the disconnector and the trigger extension.

When you do any rivet work on these, I really recommend buying a jig set. You can do it with hammers and such but that shows a pretty high level of unprofessionalism. At least I think so. Plus, it will never turn out as pretty.

There really are no difficulties with working on the AK it's pretty much what you see is what you get. If headspace is out, change the barrel. If an FCG part is broke, change that. The most difficult thing about AKs is installing the FCG parts. It's a tight squeeze and there is a lot of stuff going in there, hammer, disconnector, trigger, trip, rate reducer, springs, pins, it gets crowded quick. I will give you this advice though. When you must remove the hammer use needle nose pliers to put the spring ends behind the "T" part of the hammer and BEFORE you remove it take a 12-gauge shell and shove it over the top of the hammer and the springs.

Here you can see the springs held in place on the hammer. All that is needed is to add the shotgun shell or a zip tie to safe them up.

You can also use a zip tie, but a shotgun shell can be reused. The spring ends are sharp and will cut the hell out of you if they slide off and hit you.

There are some other things you have to be aware of, as AKs are easy to make. EVERYONE tries to make them. That means that there are a bunch of slightly dangerous AKs out there. Out of headspace, loose rivets, rivet holes elongated, receiver flats bent that nothing has been hardened. The moral of the story is be really careful when working on AKs. They are deceptively easy but just like any other firearm they can be dangerous when done wrong.

A final note on AKs, if you are planning a rental joint be very vigilant when you give some random dude an AK. They will back you up pretty good if you aren't used to it and they climb like a bitch!

CHAPTER 9

THE M16/M4

Another relatively simple gun to work on. Hell, it may even be easier than the AK! It's basically a set of Legos in gun form. Buy a part; maybe buy a special tool since every manufacturer under the sun needs their own special tool!

Anyway, buy a part, install the part, and fire away. Other than parts breakage there are only a couple things you need to worry about, bolt bounce, and parts going loose.

I just asked all the guys in the office and no one can think of any problems we have. And we shoot the hell out of it!

So, let's address bolt bounce.

Guys grab a beer because this may be a long one.

Bolt bounce is essentially when you fire a round and the bolt, on counter recoil goes into battery but "bounces" back a little bit before locking. This is bad because when the bolt comes forward enough to chamber a round it trips the full auto sear. Now that the sear has been tripped it releases the hammer. The hammer goes forward not knowing the bolt has bounced back and strikes the lower part of the carrier instead of the firing pin. This is good and bad. Good because you won't have a round fire out of battery, it's designed like that. And bad because your round you were trying to fire won't go off.

There are a lot of guns that are subject to bolt bounce and all of them I can think of have a provision to block the hammer before it hits the firing pin out of battery. Even a 10/22, which can be subject to horrible bolt bounce, has that provision built into its bolt.

So now that we know what it is how do we fix it?

Well that's where things get interesting. In theory you could just change to a heavier buffer BUT that's not always the case.

A couple different buffers and springs for the M16/M4

Things like type of ammo and gas port size can really influence how a gun fires. Even if they are from the same manufacturer! Also, how "broken in" the gun is makes a difference. Running hotter ammo in a gun is going to make recoil and counter recoil more violent and make the gun more subject to bolt bounce. Of course, you may not want to run lighter ammo for a whole host of reasons.

The best advice I can give you on this is have a good supply of various recoil buffers and springs. You may have one that has an H buffer in it that the fix is as easy as installing an H2. Or you may have one that needs an H3 and a stiffer recoil spring. The point here is be ready. No reason to make a guy wait 1-2 weeks for a part to come in when you could have swapped, test fired and had him out the door in an hour.

Here's something, I forgot to mention when I first started writing this, and I get this question a lot.

"Do you shoot steel case ammo?"

Yes, yes, I do. I have literally put tens of thousands of rounds of steel case ammo through various types of machine guns. I've never had a problem with it. Here's the deal you may break and extractor shooting it, but steel ammo is cheaper than brass and if I break an extractor or two, I'm still coming out financially better. Course you can't reload it so....

Now we address just general stuff with the M16/M4.

I mentioned loosening of parts. A big one is the castle nut on the buffer tube. It rarely gets staked and that can lead to it going loose. That has the effect of the buffer tube wiggling, just a bit; this in turn rubs against the stud on the receiver end plate and screws up the threads on the buffer tube. It's not the threads being hosed per say that is the issue. The problem is those threads are what keeps the buffer tube from rotating on the receiver end plate and thus the lower receiver. Now I'm not telling you to stake them. Because if you take it on and off it's a bitch, but you should at least use some thread locker.

The damage a loose castle nut can do if not fixed.

How about some small stuff on the M16 variants? Use a piece of tape over the hump when installing the bolt hold open pin. Also install the pin part way, install the bolt hold open catch and spring and drive pin in the rest of the way.

Most pins on the front gas block only drive one way.

Drilling the holes for the front sight gas block is a cast iron bitch. It tends to wiggle as you drill. There are jigs that help with this now and I'm here to tell you unless you are an extreme tight ass you want one. If you just don't want to pony up, then do this. Install the gas tube first and then drill from one side halfway then from the other. Drill undersize but close. After that use your reamer for the gas block pin holes (it's tapered) and finish it off.

I'm going to skip the 1919 for now and go to the M2. One because the 1919 is ugly and two because I love the M2!

CHAPTER 10

THE M2 .50 CAL

So how about the basics. The M2 is a recoil operated, belt fed, .50 caliber machine gun designed by John Browning. All those things by themselves are enough to make a stand out weapon but when you fire it you know that it's something special!

The bolt does lock on the 50 by means of a locking block that is driven up into the bottom of the bolt by a locking cam during counter recoil. The bolt is locked until, during recoil, it comes back ¾ of an inch and the breech lock depressors push the locking block down. For the rest of the cycle of operations buy your own manual ya cheapskates!

An interesting thing about the 50 is where it headspaces. It fires 1/16 inch before it is fully forward. The only time it fires fully forward is on its first round.

Headspacing the 50 is pretty simple. On the headspace and timing gage there are three pieces of metal. The large one is the headspace gage; the two smaller ones are the timing gages.

50 Cal Headspace and Timing gage set

Now your question is probably "great but how do I use it", like this my friends

Headspace Adjustment

- Screw barrel in all the way then unscrew two clicks
- Allow bolt to go forward see if the barrel rotates. If it does gun needs work, do not fire
- Charge weapon, let bolt return to battery
- Pull bolt out of battery no more than 1/16 inch.
- Insert No Go gage. It should NOT go in.

    If it does, Screw barrel IN one click at a time until No Go gage does NOT go in (After each click test headspace)

- Insert Go gage. It SHOULD go in.

If it does not, screw barrel OUT one click at a time until Go gage DOES go in (After each click test headspace)

Headspace gage between face of bolt and rear of barrel extension/barrel

Timing Adjustment

- Charge weapon, let bolt return to battery
- Insert small timing gage into gun between back of trunnion and front of barrel extension. See if gun fires. It should.
- Charge weapon,

- Insert large timing gage in same area as before. Try to fire weapon it should not.

Go timing gage inserted between rear of trunnion and front of barrel extension

You adjust timing using the timing knob in the back of the gun that contacts the trigger bar extension. Up makes it fire earlier. Down makes it fire later. Just like the headspace gage adjustment, turn see if it fires, turn see if it fires. It can be tedious but once you get the hang of it it's easy.

WARNING!!!!! If you take nothing away from this book learn this DO NOT charge an M2/M3 or any variant without the back plate on with the recoil rod assembly still in place. If you are behind it, it WILL put a hole in your chest!!!!

Inside view of an M2. The round, flat knob at top center is the timing knob with the trigger bar extension below it. To the RH side and center is the recoil rod assembly (round silver circle)

One thing I often see, though not a gunsmithing thing per say is that when carrying a 50 people grab it by the charging handle and back plate. Though not the best place to grab; the charging handle is acceptable. The back plate however is a big no-no. I have seen back plates come off using this method and it sucks.

I have seen an aircraft variant that was set up as an M2, basically, light barrel that fired fast as hell. Though cool sounding, the backplate, as I said was of the M2 variant. Not as strong as the M3. With continued usage of this there could be a catastrophic failure of the back plate while firing! This would suck beyond measure for the unlucky person firing.

The only way to fix this, short of a total rebuild with all new parts was to slow down the gun. The easiest way to do this was to add more weight. Put in a heavier bolt and the heaviest barrel that will fit in the jacket. Better to be slow than dead.

The last thing I'm going to hit on with the 50 is this. If you are firing a shit ton of rounds and you have a stoppage WAIT. The 50 is a closed bolt weapon. That means that the round is cooking in the chamber and indeed you may have a cook off. If you are about to have a cook off and you pull that bolt back at best, it will destroy the gun!

The 50 is an awesome weapon system but if you aren't careful it WILL fuck you up!

Time for the 1919, right? Nope it's still ugly.

CHAPTER 11

THE 1928 THOMPSON

The Chicago Typewriter as it was known at one time. Used by militaries and gangsters alike. The later the reason we now have the NFA and all the associated fun laws, thanks guys.

Anyway, the Thompson is another relatively easy gun to work on. It's a simple open bolt gun, that does have a semi auto provision. There is one thing that separates the Model 1928 Thompson from other blow back weapons though and that is the blish lock.

The blish lock is a locking mechanism that essentially makes the 1928 Thompson a delayed blow back weapon. It incorporates an "H" looking lock that is sandwiched between the actuator and the bolt. That being the top part and the bottom part of the bolt. The lock is free to move up and down in its area but only does so in the pathway cut into the inside forward section of the receiver.

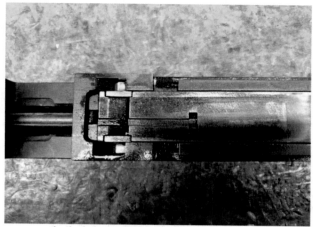

You can see the bolt in its forward position. Notice the location of the brass Blish lock.

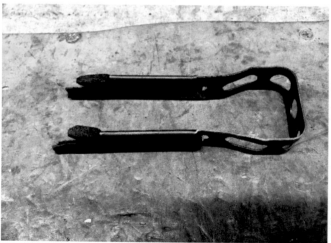

This is the oiler out of our 1928 Thompson. As an interesting aside. The gun will fire just fine without it. As a rule, it should be installed when firing though.

The disassembly of the gun is straight forward. Remove the buttstock, push the frame latch (little plunger on back of gun) down and slide back lower while holding down the trigger. Sometimes this can be a bit tight and you may have to LIGHTLY tap the lower with a mallet to remove it. That's fine but if you feel and heavy resistance STOP and see what's going on.

Take a flathead screw driver and pull the recoil spring back. You will then insert a small pin; I use a paperclip, into the hole in the recoil rod. Remove the screwdriver and push the recoil rod and buffer forward. Remove them from gun. Do not remove the paperclip unless you need to change the spring, or it will be compressed for a long pe-riod of time.

Pull bolt to rear with receiver right side up. The bolt will fall out. Push actuator forward and remove blish lock. Pull actuator to the rear and let remove from receiver.

To take out oiler squeeze sides together and remove from receiver.

Assembly is simply the reverse of disassembly.

The important things to look at here are of course any burrs or imperfections in the rubbing surfaces. Also check the oiler pads for serviceability.

One thing I forgot to mention in the first section that I will address here. When looking for burrs it's not advisable to use your fingers. Use a Qtip or a rag. It is not pleasant experience to find a piece of sharp metal with your finger!

The Thompson does have one handy thing to aid in the cleaning process. Notice the hole in the back of the receiver. Put your cleaning rod though it and screw in your brush. It's kind of nice and the only real way to clean the chamber and throat out.

About the only things I've really seen go wrong with a Thompson, that isn't just a straight parts swap, is parts coming loose from usage. Things like the forearm are pretty simple. Loctite it and press on. Things like the rear sight are a bit more challenging.

For the rear sight you will need to either resquash (it's a very technical term) the rivets or reinstall completely.

No matter which one it is you will need a proper backing bar to do it correctly. Just remember the internal part of the rivets must be absolutely flush with the receiver.

Barrel change can be a real challenge. You are sometimes dealing with a 70-year-old connection that has been through god knows what. Also, the Thompson uses squared off threads. These seem to be a bit more grippy (another technical term) than standard threads. You will want all the help you can get to do this so buy, or make, a good barrel clamp. Use the right kind of wrench that will fit on the very front of the receiver on the flats. It's also not a bad idea to use a lot of Kroil or ATF (automatic transmission fluid) and let it sit for a day or so.

Here's a helpful hint by the way, diesel and ATF mixed work wonders. Diesel has a good bit of "oiliness" to it and when combined with the ability to penetrate of the ATF it's pretty much a winning combination.

You can also try heat, but you want to be careful on how much heat you put into the receiver. I've used heat on the receiver and the barrel then when hot hit the barrel only with a bit of water. It rapidly cools the barrel and contracts it and breaks the bond. Cursing also works well too.

CHAPTER 12

THE PPSH41

There are a ton of fast and fun submachineguns, but there are none as fun as the PPSH41. Nicknamed the "Papasha" a better name would be "the popper" because it sounds like popcorn popping when it's fired! Another cool thing is that the mag will be emptied, in a proper mag dump, before the first piece of brass hits the ground.

But enough cool facts here are the particulars.

The PPSH is a Russian 7.62x25mm sub machine gun capable of both semi and fully automatic fire. It accomplishes this by means of a switch in front of the trigger. Placing the switch rearward will put the gun in "semi" placing it forward will put it in "full auto."

Here you can see the selector placed in the forward, full auto, position.

I will use this time to address something particular to rentals. I do not like handing a loaded weapon to someone and having them switch anything in the trigger guard. This includes safeties and in this case the selector switch. The reasoning is simple. A lot of times those that you give the gun to have minimal, if any weapons training. Also, they are more than likely nervous. To me this is not the time for them to be toying with anything in the trigger guard other than the trigger. It's just one more safety precaution you can take.

But back to the fun stuff.

Among one of the things I've seen with these guns is that the barrel will be drilled multiple times in the holding pin area. That means you have to mark it some kind of way to avoid installing it in the wrong way. This can lead to a bullet strike on the front of the shroud.

Another thing to watch is the buffer puck in the rear of the receiver. Due to the high rate of fire and relatively high power of the round I've found these get chewed up pretty quickly. There are aftermarket replacements for these, but I haven't tested them enough to see if they last longer.

Due to the way this is built pay extra attention to the rear lock up of the receiver. Make damn sure that the holding pin is in good shape and the ends are flared so it doesn't walk. I have seen one come apart in that area when firing and it wasn't pretty!

With rear of the receiver open we can see the buffer and the latch for the rear receiver.

You may find that some guns just don't work, and you can't figure out why. This can be a pain but here is what I've found happens a lot. In the past there have been manufacturers that have produced receiver sections for rewelding. The problem is they were a bit thicker than the original receiver sections. This has the effect of

1. Putting a "squeeze" on the bolt slowing it down and
2. Making the path of the bolt non-linear.

In other words, the bolt wiggles up and down. A couple of things can be done to fix this. Remove metal from the inside of the receiver section that's thicker (preferred way). Or weld in metal to the underside of the receiver that isn't thicker. At this point you are asking why the hell would this would be necessary. Well it depends on where the donor part was installed. If it was installed at the ejection port, and the hang up is in the section before that what is going on is that the rear section has been placed too high due to the extra thickness of the forward section. The front of your bolt is being wiggling up and down on the path and being "coned" into the front section. This could slow down the bolt enough that it produces light strikes, especially on surplus primers. So, the fix would be to build up the area on the inside of the rear receiver to the same height as the forward section. Of course, once built up you make sure the surface is smooth when done.

In either case rebuilding the entire gun may look like the best option but sometimes replacement sections just aren't available. Meaning occasionally flexibility is necessary.

CHAPTER 13

THE MP43/STG44

This is the gun everyone wants until they own one. They are THE most magazine sensitive gun I've ever dealt with. That doesn't seem bad until you find out that each STG magazine costs 500 bucks!! Buying a 500-dollar magazine and finding out it won't work in your gun is not a pleasant experience.

Late in WWII German gun designers showed Ol'Adolph a new type of battle rifle. Hitler at the time said they didn't need a replacement, especially not one that fired a smaller round.

He was OK to the idea of a new sub machine gun though.

The engineers knowing that this rifle was badly needed in the war pulled a fast one. They renamed it the MP43 (MachinenPistole 43) and started production. Sometime later Hitler started getting word about the new battle rifle and how well it was doing. I can only imagine Hitler going "What the hell?"

Anyway, it was found the new weapon that was so well received was the MP43. Hitler decided it was a good deal and had it renamed the STG44 (SturmGewehr 44).

Thus, the first Assault Rifle came to be. It set the definition for what an assault rifle is. Detachable magazine, select fire, and firing an intermediate round. This definition is still in use. Except by the news media which calls everything with a trigger an assault rifle!

Anyway, the list of problems you may see with these is long. Magazines not working. Buttstock screws coming loose and not being able to tighten them. Bolt hanging up. And last but of course the worst-case scenario, FCG parts going bad.

Starting with the worst-case scenario, FCG parts going bad or any work in the pistol grip. The chief reason for this being a not so fun proposition is that everything in there is riveted in. Also guess what you can't find anymore. that's right STG44 FCG rivets. So right off the bat rivets or a holding pin must be made.

I don't know if you have ever actually looked into the FCG of an MP44 but for now gaze into it and despair. It is chocked full of springs and parts. The best advice I can give you if you must work on one is take lots of pictures and grab an exploded diagram. It's just something you are going to have to tackle and take your time.

Interior view of the STG44 FCG.

Buttstock issues are a little easier to deal with. Normally what happens is that since the screws are screwed directly into the wood they elongate over time and get loose. You will also see most times the screws holes are a dark color from oil seepage. Unfortunately, there isn't a good way to get oil out of the screw holes, but it can still be fixed.

What I've found that works is to score the wood in the screw hole to make it a bit bigger and jagged. Take stock bedding compound and fill the hole up. Screw the metal plate back on and let it set according to the until the bedding compound has cured. So far, the ones I've done haven't loosened up or cracked out. Something I was originally worried about. A quick note on this. If you coat the screw with a fine coating of oil, it shouldn't stick to the bedding compound. If you fail to coat the screw, the compound with bond to it and I wouldn't count on getting that screw out, ever.

Now the bolt hanging up covers a ton of ground. I have one that is doing that now and for the life of me I can't figure out why. I'll get it but that may be for another book.

Normally it's our old friend carbon fouling that raises its ugly head but there are some other issues that happen. One could be wearing on the hammer which causes the hammer not to set in the sear. When that happens, the hammer can become trapped between the area between carrier and bolt. Of course, this leads to FCG work which is no fun at all.

Another issue is when the charging handle breaks off. This sucks and the only real way to fix it is to get a new charging handle, yes they are being made now! Or you could get a new carrier for 1000 bucks! The problem is that there is a shaft on the charging handle that runs through the body of the carrier. When this breaks there is nowhere to weld on it. You can't just weld the handle back on as the area for it in the receiver is very small. It can be done but the repair doesn't last too long.

CHAPTER 14

OK DAMNIT...... THE 1919

First off, I am biased against this gun. Not because it doesn't work great, it does. But because it just lacks style points!

The 1919s design originally was a water-cooled weapon called the 1917. The 1919 being air cooled. It has been used by a ton of countries, in a ton of conflicts, in many different calibers. You will likely see this gun in the 7.26x51 and the 7.62x54r calibers. While it was chambered in US .30cal and 8mm those cartridges are getting hard to find and very expensive to shoot full auto.

The action is of a gas assisted blow back somewhat like the MG43/42. After firing a round the barrel, barrel extension, and bolt move to the rear, gas is trapped in the front of the barrel in the barrel bearing.

Now there are two types of barrel bearing. The variety that you can swap the booster and the variety that it is integral to the bearing. We will be dealing with the former.

The barrel booster that screws onto the bearing has different size holes to adjust how much or how little gas gets used. This will need to be changed depending on caliber used.

Head spacing should be accomplished with the head-space and timing gauge. It's simple to use and a lot like how the 50 headspaces the big difference is that the 1919 fires when barrel extension is touching the trunnion. So, what you will do is this.

Pull the charging handle back about 3/4" to the rear. Between the rear of the barrel and front of the bolt insert your headspace gauge (.125" one). Now simply turn the barrel in until the gage is tight between them. Back it off one click, and you're done! Now this is for a brand-new gun with brand new parts. The one you are probably working on is nowhere near new so you may have to adjust that a tad one way or the other. Basically, you will have to experiment a bit. Now there are a couple other ways to do it but I'm not going to mention those here. Let's just stick to the "by the book" thing for now.

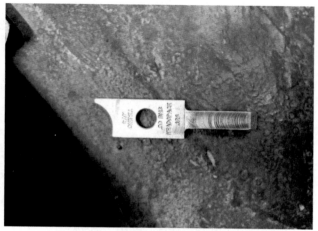
1919 headspace and timing gauge

Timing is equally easy. Pop your .120" gauge in between the trunnion and the barrel extension, after you have already charged the weapon. Try to fire, it should not. Next try the .030" gage. On this one it should fire.

Now here's the tricky part.

To adjust timing, you will need to bend the trigger bar.

If gun is firing too fast and needs adjustment, you will have to bend the dovetail of the trigger bar upward. Vice versa for a gun firing to slow.

Don't bend to much! Only do small increments at a time.

When you go to remove the back plate, you must lock the recoil spring in the bolt. You do this by pulling the bolt to the rear and turning the recoil spring guide 90 degrees.

This locks the recoil spring in place. At this time the spring is COMPRESSED so do not get behind it!!

I usually cycle the bolt by hand a couple times to ensure its not going to fly out the instant I take off the back plate. Better safe than sorry and all that.

The little slotted head, showing out the backplate, in the middle of the photo is the Recoil spring guide. Make damn sure this is correctly locked in the bolt before removing the back plate

When you have the bolt out of the gun with the recoil spring in it do not point it at anyone. Basically, treat it as a gun.

CHAPTER 15

THE MOST BEAUTIFUL GUN IN THE WORLD, THE MG34

This is the gun that started me liking machine guns. The German Machinegewehr 34, or MG34 as it is known was the first successful General-Purpose Machine Gun or GPMG. This basically means it could fill several roles. Light machinegun on the bipod or medium or heavy machine gun on the Lafette tripod. It could be fired semi or full auto. It had a good rate of fire at 1000 rounds per minute of 7.92x57 (8mm) ammunition.

It was a mechanical marvel incorporating massive amounts of machining to manufacture and it can be an absolute nightmare to work on!

When I say it's difficult to work on what I mean is there are a ton of parts in it and the tolerances in the gun are VERY tight! The bolt alone has 27 parts!

MG34 bolt in all its glory. It's not difficult to work on but there are 27 parts that could go bad on it!

Remember virtually all the parts in any MG34 have been used and abused for over 70 years. That's a lot of rounds to fire and when things mess up it can be a challenge to find out exactly what part is going bad.

Remember when I mentioned John Baums translated MG manuals? This is one area where they are invaluable! Trust me it's money well spent.

Most of the problems I've seen with the MG34 amount to bad parts so it's an easy parts swap thing but there is one thing that is maddening that you will see if you work on them. Sometimes certain bolts and barrels will headspace fine but not work with each other. I have no idea why this happens, but it does. So, what you do is go to the range with a couple different bolts and barrels and when you find a pair that works well together either mark them or write down the combo. This will save you a great deal of pain later.

Another thing is the barrel return plunger and spring. I have seen those go bad and there are two styles of them, long and short plunger. You will need to make sure that you are installing the correct one or the gun won't work.

One other thing that will go bad over time is the booster cone. This being the part under the flash hider that traps gas to aide in recoil. These wear over time and will need to be replaced. The standard hole size on these is 11.5mm too big and you don't have enough recoil to make the gun function correctly. I've never seen one too small but there are .308 ones out there that do have a smaller hole and reduced pressure area (the inside of the booster). If your 34 is running at 42 speeds I'd look there first.

MG34 booster, the hole should be 11.5mm on a new booster. These carbon up fast so stay on top of the cleaning.

On rewelded guns I've seen bolts hang up in the receiver channel. As I've said the tolerances in a 34 are stupid tight. There should not be much play in the bolt down the receiver channel. Of course, stoppages of the bolt when moving it by hand are a big indicator of a problem. If you do suspect the receiver may have something to do with that, you will need to apply some layout blue and run the bolt by hand and see where it hangs. The layout blue will help you find the specific areas that the bolt is rubbing and give you a head start on what the next process is. The next step may be just filing a small area, or it may be a complete rebuild!

Rear of the MG34 with the bolt installed to show how tight the tolerances are. There isn't a lot of room for error when rebuilding one. Even a bit of dirt will make the thing not run.

In short, the MG34 isn't a bad gun but it does have some quirks. It doesn't take much to gum one up and there are so many parts trouble shooting can be a challenge. That having been said when they run right it is a sweet gun!

CHAPTER 16

THE 1918 BAR

The BAR is a brick of a gun but it's a good shooter and even more than that the weapon has an iconic image from its use in WWII. You don't see them as much as you used to due to the cost and availability of 30-06 ammo, and because a BAR is a very expensive gun!

It's a gas operated full auto weapon that had 2 different settings for full auto, 600RPM and 350RPM. Why they decided to have two full auto settings is lost on me. There is also a safe setting but that is blocked off by a pin you need to depress to engage it! Strange stuff indeed. The gas system does have three gas settings.

The locking mechanism is accomplished by the back of the bolt tilting up into a locking shoulder.

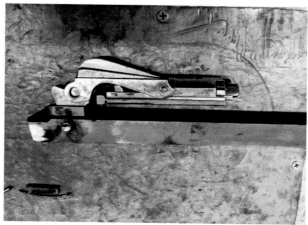

Here we see the bolt and carrier assembled and, in the orientation, they would be if they were in the gun. These parts are damn near bomb proof, but they can and do break.

The problems I've heard of with the gun, mechanical problems that is, not the standard "it's not a good gun" problems, are a bad buffer, chamber fouling, and bolt sticking.

The buffer is easy enough to fix if you can find the parts. There is also a special tool required for disassembly. One can use a punch of the correct size to take it apart but it's not technically correct.

Chamber fouling or burs in this gun can be bad, as it's not easy to get a hone to the chamber to polish it. Basically, if you can get to it, use a long chamber hone with the gun completely disassembled. The other alternative is to take the barrel off. Something that's not fun!

Now bolt sticking can be caused by many things but one I've seen is the bolt guide spring has broken and caused all sorts of havoc. This one will mar up a bunch of stuff usually so break out those files!

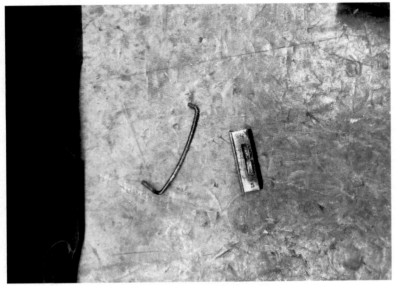

Bolt guide spring and bolt guide.

And of course, our old friend, carbon build up comes into play. You will see it in the gas tube but more likely the cause is the buildup in the gas tube cap where you change your gas setting.

For the gas tube, an appropriately sized brass bore brush will work. Soak it in carbon remover and go to town!

As to the cap that will need to be disassembled and cleaned. I soak it overnight in carbon remover and it makes the job much easier.

Here is the Gas tube cap, assembled. Getting the carbon build up out of this can be a bit of a challenge depending on how long the owner has let it go between cleanings.

CHAPTER 17

TEST FIRE

After you've fixed the gun you need to test out right? Well easy enough just shoot it!

There are a couple things I do though.

First, I'll cycle the action by hand to make sure everything seems to work right. After that I'll load one round. Fire it off and check the action again. Next, load 3 and full auto them. If that works, the next step will be to load a belt (or a mag) and cycle between three rounds full auto and three rounds semi. If it still good to go, I'll do a mag dump and call it good! Of course, there is a posttest fire inspection too.

CHAPTER 18

DEALING WITH THE UNKNOWN

You may have noticed that I didn't mention a ton of fixes for each gun. There are a couple reasons for that. As I've said I don't want to write a "do this like this" book and honestly there are so many possibilities that I don't think a book could be written covering all the possible breaks and fixes of each gun listed let alone all the machine guns out there! Instead I am hoping to guide an already knowledgeable gunsmith to the land of full autos. This can be both rewarding and a ton of fun! Of course, there can be a ton of frustrations as well.

A couple of the reasons that folks don't go into full auto repair more is there is nowhere to learn it. I think this is a huge detriment as people can be very apprehensive about working on something they have never worked on before.

An even bigger reason, I think, is the cost of a transferable weapon. You are looking at an easy cost of 10,000 dollars to start! That can be very intimidating! But look at it this way. What separates a gunsmith from a run of the mill guy who is good with his hands is the WILLINGNESS to get in there and start taking things apart! In other words,

you aren't afraid to "get your hands dirty" on this stuff because you KNOW damn well that you can fix it. Why
shouldn't this attitude carry over to the machine gun world?
No reason right.

Made in the USA
Middletown, DE
22 October 2022

13280219R00058